Alexander Astremsky

Observation Notebook

Story-Flash System **Book 3**

Copyright

Copyright © 2020 Alexander Astremsky. "
All rights are reserved and protected by copyright law. No part of this book may be copied or reproduced in any form or by whatever means – electronic, mechanical, including photocopying, recording, posting on the Internet and corporate networks for private and public usage – without written permission, with the exception for brief quotation in critical articles and reviews. Coordinated usage of material is made with the author.

About The Author

Alexander Astremsky is a writer, screenwriter, author of the science fiction series *Intangibleworld*, and an economic novel and board games *Money Rules*. He is also the owner of Astremsky Marketing, a company that operates in five countries and develops presentation materials and corporate magazines. Alexander is a professional speaker and the author of online articles on plot development read by over 500 thousand people.

About The Observation Notebook

The Story-Flash Observation Notebook is an indispensable assistant to any writer or screenwriter. It is based on exercises from the book *Story-Flash: Step-by-Step Technology of Plot Development* and allows you to make a thorough analysis of the movies you watch.

- What is the protagonist's goal?
- Which of his actions make us like him?
- What is his flaw?
- Why do we dislike the antagonist?
- What are the main conflicts in the movie?
- What threat hangs over the protagonist?
- What are the main turning points?
- At what point does the protagonist have his crisis?

Answering these and many other questions allows you to understand what the films you analyze are "made of."

By writing your observations in this Notebook you will improve your ability to create exciting stories. You can also record valuable ideas for your own stories in here.

The Story-Flash Observation Notebook makes a great gift for beginners and even experienced writers, especially together with the first two books of the *Story-Flash* series.

Film #1
Title

_____

_____

Part 1

1. Observation: Protagonist's Goals and Intentions

- *Describe the protagonist's goal.*
- *What does he want to achieve?*
- *Describe his intentions (what he wants to do and what he is trying to avoid).*

2. Observation: Protagonist's Skills

List the knowledge, skills and abilities of the protagonist.

3. Observation: Protagonist's Tools

List the tools of the protagonist in the movie.

4. Observation: Emotional Wound

- *Determine the "emotional wound" of the protagonist.*
- *Describe how it affects his personality and actions.*

5. Observation: Protagonist's Flaw

- *Find and name the protagonist's flaw.*
- *Describe how this flaw prevents him from achieving his goals.*

6. Observation: Creating the Antagonist

- *Who is the antagonist in this film?*
- *Describe his goal precisely. What does he want to achieve?*
- *Describe the antagonist's intentions (what he wants to do and what he is he trying to avoid).*

7. Observation: Antagonist's Abilities

Describe what makes the antagonist invincible and unpredictable.

8. Observation: Reason for Confrontation

- *What is the main conflict between the protagonist and the antagonist?*
- *Determine the reason for the protagonist's opposition to the antagonist.*
- *Why does one resist the other so furiously?*

9. Observation: A Spoke in the Wheel

List how the antagonist puts a spoke in the protagonist's wheel. What barriers does he create?

10. Observation: Goals of the Secondary Characters

- *Make a list of several friends of the protagonist in the movie. Describe their intentions and goals.*
- *List the several enemies of the protagonist.*
- *Describe their intentions and goals.*

11. Observation: Secondary Conflicts

Describe the secondary conflicts of this film.

12. Observation: Antipathy towards the Antagonist

- *Describe the negative actions taken by the antagonist.*
- *Specify why these actions cause feelings of dislike towards him.*

13. Observation: Punishment for the Antagonist

- *Describe the antagonist's punishments.*
- *What exactly makes the viewer rejoice?*
- *How does the justice triumph?*

14. Observation: Reward for the Protagonist

- *Describe what the protagonist receives for his hard work.*
- *Specify why it is valuable and important to him.*

15. Observation: Threats

- *Describe the threats that are hanging over the hero.*
- *Specify the greatest danger.*

16. Observation: Protagonist's Change

Describe how exactly the protagonist changes in the movie.

17. Observation: Secondary Line

- *Describe the secondary plot lines of this film.*
- *Determine how they create additional depth for the story.*

18. Observation: Protagonist's Development

- *Describe who (or what) helps the hero acquire new knowledge and experience.*
- *Why is this knowledge important?*
- *What difference does it make for the events of the story?*

19. Observation: Legend

- *If the film includes a legend, describe it in several sentences.*
- *Indicate how it immerses the viewer into the story.*

20. Observation: Primary Situation

- *Describe the primary situation of this film.*
- *Try to do it in five sentences.*

21. Observation: Plot Outline

Recall and describe the plot of the movie dividing it into three parts — the beginning, the middle and the end.

Part 2

1. Observation: Exposition

- *Watch the beginning of the movie.*
- *Describe the exposition in several sentences.*
- *Name the actions used by the screenwriter to introduce the protagonist to us.*

2. Observation: Inciting Incident

- *Find the "inciting incident" in the film.*
- *Describe how this incident sends the protagonist on a journey.*
- *How exactly does he get pulled into the "game"?*

3. Observation: Orientation Period

- *Determine when the orientation period begins and ends in the movie.*
- *What does the protagonist learn during this period?*

4. Observation: First Plot Point

- *Find the "first plot point" in the film.*
- *Describe why this event is a powerful impetus for the entire second act.*

5. Observation: Adjustment Period

- *Determine when the adjustment period begins and ends in the movie.*
- *What does the protagonist do during this period?*
- *How does he adjust to the circumstances?*

6. Observation: Main Turning Point

- *Find the "main turning point" in the film.*
- *Describe why this is the point where the hero becomes more of a master of the situation rather than a person who is going with the flow.*
- *Describe how the protagonist "burns all his bridges" (if that does take).*

_____
_____
_____
_____
_____
_____
_____
_____
_____
_____
_____

7. Observation: Action Period

- *Determine when the action period begins and when it ends.*
- *What does the protagonist do during this period? Describe all his actions.*
- *Specify HOW the principle of "every action has an equal and opposite reaction" is used to create the confrontation between the protagonist and antagonist.*
- *What does the antagonist do to react to the protagonist's actions?*

8. Observation: Second Plot Point

- *Determine the "second plot point" in the film.*
- *Describe why this event is a "big failure."*
- *Determine what makes this event a catalyst for conflict and tension.*

9. Observation: Protagonist's Crisis

- *Determine the protagonist's crisis in the film.*
- *Describe the choice that the hero has to make.*
- *What makes this moment a test of the hero's willpower and integrity?*
- *How exactly does the protagonist's modus operandi change because of this crisis?*

10. Observation: Final Battle

- *Describe the final battle in the film.*
- *What ideals clash in this battle (lies vs. truth, being dependent on a rich husband vs. freedom, friendship vs. betrayal, etc.)?*

11. Observation: Climax

- *Determine the climax of the film.*
- *Describe the victory of the principles that the protagonist was fighting for (if it is not a drama and the hero is victorious).*

12. Observation: Resolution

- *Find the moment that demonstrates the value of the victory for the protagonist. Describe how he enjoys the win (if it is shown).*
- *How can we see that the victory is final, and the evil is not likely to come back?*
- *Describe the moment (the scene) that demonstrates the change in the protagonist's life after his victory over evil (if shown).*
- *Does this movie show that the hero's ideals are now a reality? If so, how?*

13. Observation: Create the Timeline

- *Create the TIMELINE for the film you have chosen.*

Yes, this is not going to be easy or quick, but this Observation will allow you to see the entire structure of the film. This will help you gain a "professional's point of view.

Would you like to learn how to "see" the structure of successful films? Then do this!

_____
_____
_____
_____
_____
_____
_____
_____
_____
_____

14. Observation: Episode Plan

Create the episode plan for the film you have chosen.

15. Observation: Elements that Advance the Plot

Find the elements that advance the plot in each episode of your episode plan.

16. Observation: List of Episodes

Make a list of all the episodes in the film you have chosen and give them names.

Part 3

1. Observation: Character's Function

Choose three characters from the movie you have just watched.

Describe each of them as follows:

- *What are his intentions?*
- *Does he interfere with the protagonist achieving his goal or does he help him? (Unless this is the protagonist.)*
- *What methods does he use to pursue his intentions?*
- *What is his role in the story?*
- *Why was he introduced into the story?*

----

2. Observation: Character's Goal

Describe the GOALS of the three characters you have chosen.

3. Observation: Motivation

- *Describe the MOTIVATION of the three characters you have chosen.*
- *Why must each of them perform his function?*
- *WHAt is his reason for that?*
- *Determine whether the motivation of those characters changes as the story unfolds.*

4. Observation: Character's "Heaven"

- *Describe the "HEAVEN" of the characters you have chosen the way you see it.*
- *Answer these questions about each character: What does he dream about? What does he strive for?*

5. Observation: Character's "Hell"

- *Describe the "HELL" of the characters you have chosen the way you see it.*
- *Answer these questions about each character: What is his biggest fear?*
- *What is he trying to avoid at all costs?*
- *What will happen if he doesn't reach his goal or solve the main problem?*

6. Observation: Character's Emotional wound

Describe the emotional wounds of the characters you have chosen.

_____
_____
_____
_____
_____
_____
_____
_____
_____
_____
_____
_____
_____
_____
_____
_____

7. Observation: Internal Conflict

Describe the internal conflicts of the characters you have chosen.

8. Observation: Character's Strengths

- *Describe strong points of the chosen characters.*
- *Determine which of these strong points help each character achieve their goals.*

9. Observation: Character's Weaknesses

- *Describe the weak points of each character you have chosen.*
- *Determine how these weak points impede each character in achieving his goals.*

10. Observation: Character's Characteristics

- *Identify and describe the internal characteristics of each character you have chosen.*
- *Do the internal characteristics influence the story?*
- *Identify and describe the external characteristics of each character.*

11. Observation: External Image

Describe in detail the appearance of the characters you have chosen.

12. Observation: Conflicts

- *Describe the conflicts that involve the characters you have chosen.*
- *Specify the reason for each conflict.*

13. Observation: Character's Personal Growth

- *Determine whether the characters you have chosen experience personal growth. If so, describe it.*
- *Describe the reasons for this personal growth.*

Part 4

1. Observation: The Main Question

Identify and write down the "main question" of the movie.

2. Observation: The Hooks

- *Find and describe the "hooks" in the movie.*
- *Write down the question the viewers are asking themselves as a result of each "hook."*

3. Observation: The Keys

- *Find the "keys" in the movie.*
- *Describe why the protagonist would not be able to move further without at least one of the keys, in other words, why the plot would get stuck in that case.*

4. Observation: Obtaining the Keys

- *Determine which "keys" the protagonist gets easily and which he obtains with great difficulty.*
- *Describe the protagonist's RISK and dangers he had to face in those scenes in which the key was hard to get.*
- *Think of some other ways that would make obtaining the "keys" even more complicated.*

5. Observation: Pressure of Circumstances

Describe how the "increasing pressure of the circumstances" is represented in the movie.

6. Observation: Surprises and Unexpected Twists

Describe the surprises and unexpected twists in the movie.

Film #2 Title

_____

_____

Part 1

1. Observation: Protagonist's Goals and Intentions

- *Describe the protagonist's goal.*
- *What does he want to achieve?*
- *Describe his intentions (what he wants to do and what he is trying to avoid).*

2. Observation: Protagonist's Skills

List the knowledge, skills and abilities of the protagonist.

3. Observation: Protagonist's Tools

List the tools of the protagonist in the movie.

4. Observation: Emotional Wound

- *Determine the "emotional wound" of the protagonist.*
- *Describe how it affects his personality and actions.*

5. Observation: Protagonist's Flaw

- *Find and name the protagonist's flaw.*
- *Describe how this flaw prevents him from achieving his goals.*

6. Observation: Creating the Antagonist

- *Who is the antagonist in this film?*
- *Describe his goal precisely. What does he want to achieve?*
- *Describe the antagonist's intentions (what he wants to do and what he is he trying to avoid).*

7. Observation: Antagonist's Abilities

Describe what makes the antagonist invincible and unpredictable.

8. Observation: Reason for Confrontation

- *What is the main conflict between the protagonist and the antagonist?*
- *Determine the reason for the protagonist's opposition to the antagonist.*
- *Why does one resist the other so furiously?*

_____
_____
_____
_____
_____
_____
_____
_____
_____
_____
_____
_____
_____
_____

9. Observation: A Spoke in the Wheel

List how the antagonist puts a spoke in the protagonist's wheel. What barriers does he create?

10. Observation: Goals of the Secondary Characters

- *Make a list of several friends of the protagonist in the movie. Describe their intentions and goals.*
- *List the several enemies of the protagonist.*
- *Describe their intentions and goals.*

_____
_____
_____
_____
_____
_____
_____
_____
_____
_____
_____
_____
_____
_____

11. Observation: Secondary Conflicts

Describe the secondary conflicts of this film.

12. Observation: Antipathy towards the Antagonist

- *Describe the negative actions taken by the antagonist.*
- *Specify why these actions cause feelings of dislike towards him.*

_____
_____
_____
_____
_____
_____
_____
_____
_____
_____
_____
_____
_____
_____

13. Observation: Punishment for the Antagonist

- *Describe the antagonist's punishments.*
- *What exactly makes the viewer rejoice?*
- *How does the justice triumph?*

14. Observation: Reward for the Protagonist

- *Describe what the protagonist receives for his hard work.*
- *Specify why it is valuable and important to him.*

15. Observation: Threats

- *Describe the threats that are hanging over the hero.*
- *Specify the greatest danger.*

16. Observation: Protagonist's Change

Describe how exactly the protagonist changes in the movie.

17. Observation: Secondary Line

- *Describe the secondary plot lines of this film.*
- *Determine how they create additional depth for the story.*

18. Observation: Protagonist's Development

- *Describe who (or what) helps the hero acquire new knowledge and experience.*
- *Why is this knowledge important?*
- *What difference does it make for the events of the story?*

19. Observation: Legend

- *If the film includes a legend, describe it in several sentences.*
- *Indicate how it immerses the viewer into the story.*

20. Observation: Primary Situation

- *Describe the primary situation of this film.*
- *Try to do it in five sentences.*

21. Observation: Plot Outline

Recall and describe the plot of the movie dividing it into three parts — the beginning, the middle and the end.

Part 2

1. Observation: Exposition

- *Watch the beginning of the movie.*
- *Describe the exposition in several sentences.*
- *Name the actions used by the screenwriter to introduce the protagonist to us.*

2. Observation: Inciting Incident

- *Find the "inciting incident" in the film.*
- *Describe how this incident sends the protagonist on a journey.*
- *How exactly does he get pulled into the "game"?*

3. Observation: Orientation Period

- *Determine when the orientation period begins and ends in the movie.*
- *What does the protagonist learn during this period?*

_____
_____
_____
_____
_____
_____
_____
_____
_____
_____
_____
_____
_____
_____

4. Observation: First Plot Point

- *Find the "first plot point" in the film.*
- *Describe why this event is a powerful impetus for the entire second act.*

5. Observation: Adjustment Period

- *Determine when the adjustment period begins and ends in the movie.*
- *What does the protagonist do during this period?*
- *How does he adjust to the circumstances?*

6. Observation: Main Turning Point

- *Find the "main turning point" in the film.*
- *Describe why this is the point where the hero becomes more of a master of the situation rather than a person who is going with the flow.*
- *Describe how the protagonist "burns all his bridges" (if that does take).*

7. Observation: Action Period

- *Determine when the action period begins and when it ends.*
- *What does the protagonist do during this period? Describe all his actions.*
- *Specify HOW the principle of "every action has an equal and opposite reaction" is used to create the confrontation between the protagonist and antagonist.*
- *What does the antagonist do to react to the protagonist's actions?*

8. Observation: Second Plot Point

- *Determine the "second plot point" in the film.*
- *Describe why this event is a "big failure."*
- *Determine what makes this event a catalyst for conflict and tension.*

9. Observation: Protagonist's Crisis

- *Determine the protagonist's crisis in the film.*
- *Describe the choice that the hero has to make.*
- *What makes this moment a test of the hero's willpower and integrity?*
- *How exactly does the protagonist's modus operandi change because of this crisis?*

10. Observation: Final Battle

- *Describe the final battle in the film.*
- *What ideals clash in this battle (lies vs. truth, being dependent on a rich husband vs. freedom, friendship vs. betrayal, etc.)?*

11. Observation: Climax

- *Determine the climax of the film.*
- *Describe the victory of the principles that the protagonist was fighting for (if it is not a drama and the hero is victorious).*

12. Observation: Resolution

- *Find the moment that demonstrates the value of the victory for the protagonist. Describe how he enjoys the win (if it is shown).*
- *How can we see that the victory is final, and the evil is not likely to come back?*
- *Describe the moment (the scene) that demonstrates the change in the protagonist's life after his victory over evil (if shown).*
- *Does this movie show that the hero's ideals are now a reality? If so, how?*

13. Observation: Create the Timeline

- *Create the TIMELINE for the film you have chosen.*

Yes, this is not going to be easy or quick, but this Observation will allow you to see the entire structure of the film. This will help you gain a "professional's point of view.

Would you like to learn how to "see" the structure of successful films? Then do this!

14. Observation: Episode Plan

Create the episode plan for the film you have chosen.

15. Observation: Elements that Advance the Plot

Find the elements that advance the plot in each episode of your episode plan.

16. Observation: List of Episodes

Make a list of all the episodes in the film you have chosen and give them names.

Part 3

1. Observation: Character's Function

Choose three characters from the movie you have just watched.

Describe each of them as follows:

- *What are his intentions?*
- *Does he interfere with the protagonist achieving his goal or does he help him? (Unless this is the protagonist.)*
- *What methods does he use to pursue his intentions?*
- *What is his role in the story?*
- *Why was he introduced into the story?*

2. Observation: Character's Goal

Describe the GOALS of the three characters you have chosen.

3. Observation: Motivation

- *Describe the MOTIVATION of the three characters you have chosen.*
- *Why must each of them perform his function?*
- *WHAt is his reason for that?*
- *Determine whether the motivation of those characters changes as the story unfolds.*

4. Observation: Character's "Heaven"

- *Describe the "HEAVEN" of the characters you have chosen the way you see it.*
- *Answer these questions about each character: What does he dream about? What does he strive for?*

5. Observation: Character's "Hell"

- *Describe the "HELL" of the characters you have chosen the way you see it.*
- *Answer these questions about each character: What is his biggest fear?*
- *What is he trying to avoid at all costs?*
- *What will happen if he doesn't reach his goal or solve the main problem?*

6. Observation: Character's Emotional wound

Describe the emotional wounds of the characters you have chosen.

7. Observation: Internal Conflict

Describe the internal conflicts of the characters you have chosen.

8. Observation: Character's Strengths

- *Describe strong points of the chosen characters.*
- *Determine which of these strong points help each character achieve their goals.*

9. Observation: Character's Weaknesses

- *Describe the weak points of each character you have chosen.*
- *Determine how these weak points impede each character in achieving his goals.*

10. Observation: Character's Characteristics

- *Identify and describe the internal characteristics of each character you have chosen.*
- *Do the internal characteristics influence the story?*
- *Identify and describe the external characteristics of each character.*

_____
_____
_____
_____
_____
_____
_____
_____
_____
_____
_____
_____

11. Observation: External Image

Describe in detail the appearance of the characters you have chosen.

12. Observation: Conflicts

- *Describe the conflicts that involve the characters you have chosen.*
- *Specify the reason for each conflict.*

_____
_____
_____
_____
_____
_____
_____
_____
_____
_____
_____
_____
_____
_____
_____
_____

13. Observation: Character's Personal Growth

- *Determine whether the characters you have chosen experience personal growth. If so, describe it.*
- *Describe the reasons for this personal growth.*

Part 4

1. Observation: The Main Question

Identify and write down the "main question" of the movie.

2. Observation: The Hooks

- *Find and describe the "hooks" in the movie.*
- *Write down the question the viewers are asking themselves as a result of each "hook."*

3. Observation: The Keys

- *Find the "keys" in the movie.*
- *Describe why the protagonist would not be able to move further without at least one of the keys, in other words, why the plot would get stuck in that case.*

_____
_____
_____
_____
_____
_____
_____
_____
_____
_____
_____
_____
_____
_____

4. Observation: Obtaining the Keys

- *Determine which "keys" the protagonist gets easily and which he obtains with great difficulty.*
- *Describe the protagonist's RISK and dangers he had to face in those scenes in which the key was hard to get.*
- *Think of some other ways that would make obtaining the "keys" even more complicated.*

5. Observation: Pressure of Circumstances

Describe how the "increasing pressure of the circumstances" is represented in the movie.

_____
_____
_____
_____
_____
_____
_____
_____
_____
_____
_____
_____
_____
_____
_____
_____

6. Observation: Surprises and Unexpected Twists

Describe the surprises and unexpected twists in the movie.

Film #3 Title

_____

_____

Part 1

1. Observation: Protagonist's Goals and Intentions

- *Describe the protagonist's goal.*
- *What does he want to achieve?*
- *Describe his intentions (what he wants to do and what he is trying to avoid).*

2. Observation: Protagonist's Skills

List the knowledge, skills and abilities of the protagonist.

3. Observation: Protagonist's Tools

List the tools of the protagonist in the movie.

4. Observation: Emotional Wound

- *Determine the "emotional wound" of the protagonist.*
- *Describe how it affects his personality and actions.*

----

5. Observation: Protagonist's Flaw

- *Find and name the protagonist's flaw.*
- *Describe how this flaw prevents him from achieving his goals.*

6. Observation: Creating the Antagonist

- *Who is the antagonist in this film?*
- *Describe his goal precisely. What does he want to achieve?*
- *Describe the antagonist's intentions (what he wants to do and what he is he trying to avoid).*

7. Observation: Antagonist's Abilities

Describe what makes the antagonist invincible and unpredictable.

8. Observation: Reason for Confrontation

- *What is the main conflict between the protagonist and the antagonist?*
- *Determine the reason for the protagonist's opposition to the antagonist.*
- *Why does one resist the other so furiously?*

_____
_____
_____
_____
_____
_____
_____
_____
_____
_____
_____
_____
_____

9. Observation: A Spoke in the Wheel

List how the antagonist puts a spoke in the protagonist's wheel. What barriers does he create?

10. Observation: Goals of the Secondary Characters

- *Make a list of several friends of the protagonist in the movie. Describe their intentions and goals.*
- *List the several enemies of the protagonist.*
- *Describe their intentions and goals.*

11. Observation: Secondary Conflicts

Describe the secondary conflicts of this film.

12. Observation: Antipathy towards the Antagonist

- *Describe the negative actions taken by the antagonist.*
- *Specify why these actions cause feelings of dislike towards him.*

13. Observation: Punishment for the Antagonist

- *Describe the antagonist's punishments.*
- *What exactly makes the viewer rejoice?*
- *How does the justice triumph?*

14. Observation: Reward for the Protagonist

- *Describe what the protagonist receives for his hard work.*
- *Specify why it is valuable and important to him.*

_____
_____
_____
_____
_____
_____
_____
_____
_____
_____
_____
_____
_____
_____
_____

15. Observation: Threats

- *Describe the threats that are hanging over the hero.*
- *Specify the greatest danger.*

16. Observation: Protagonist's Change

Describe how exactly the protagonist changes in the movie.

17. Observation: Secondary Line

- *Describe the secondary plot lines of this film.*
- *Determine how they create additional depth for the story.*

18. Observation: Protagonist's Development

- *Describe who (or what) helps the hero acquire new knowledge and experience.*
- *Why is this knowledge important?*
- *What difference does it make for the events of the story?*

19. Observation: Legend

- *If the film includes a legend, describe it in several sentences.*
- *Indicate how it immerses the viewer into the story.*

20. Observation: Primary Situation

- *Describe the primary situation of this film.*
- *Try to do it in five sentences.*

21. Observation: Plot Outline

Recall and describe the plot of the movie dividing it into three parts — the beginning, the middle and the end.

Part 2

1. Observation: Exposition

- *Watch the beginning of the movie.*
- *Describe the exposition in several sentences.*
- *Name the actions used by the screenwriter to introduce the protagonist to us.*

2. Observation: Inciting Incident

- *Find the "inciting incident" in the film.*
- *Describe how this incident sends the protagonist on a journey.*
- *How exactly does he get pulled into the "game"?*

3. Observation: Orientation Period

- *Determine when the orientation period begins and ends in the movie.*
- *What does the protagonist learn during this period?*

4. Observation: First Plot Point

- *Find the "first plot point" in the film.*
- *Describe why this event is a powerful impetus for the entire second act.*

5. Observation: Adjustment Period

- *Determine when the adjustment period begins and ends in the movie.*
- *What does the protagonist do during this period?*
- *How does he adjust to the circumstances?*

6. Observation: Main Turning Point

- *Find the "main turning point" in the film.*
- *Describe why this is the point where the hero becomes more of a master of the situation rather than a person who is going with the flow.*
- *Describe how the protagonist "burns all his bridges" (if that does take).*

7. Observation: Action Period

- *Determine when the action period begins and when it ends.*
- *What does the protagonist do during this period? Describe all his actions.*
- *Specify HOW the principle of "every action has an equal and opposite reaction" is used to create the confrontation between the protagonist and antagonist.*
- *What does the antagonist do to react to the protagonist's actions?*

8. Observation: Second Plot Point

- *Determine the "second plot point" in the film.*
- *Describe why this event is a "big failure."*
- *Determine what makes this event a catalyst for conflict and tension.*

----

9. Observation: Protagonist's Crisis

- *Determine the protagonist's crisis in the film.*
- *Describe the choice that the hero has to make.*
- *What makes this moment a test of the hero's willpower and integrity?*
- *How exactly does the protagonist's modus operandi change because of this crisis?*

10. Observation: Final Battle

- *Describe the final battle in the film.*
- *What ideals clash in this battle (lies vs. truth, being dependent on a rich husband vs. freedom, friendship vs. betrayal, etc.)?*

11. Observation: Climax

- *Determine the climax of the film.*
- *Describe the victory of the principles that the protagonist was fighting for (if it is not a drama and the hero is victorious).*

12. Observation: Resolution

- *Find the moment that demonstrates the value of the victory for the protagonist. Describe how he enjoys the win (if it is shown).*
- *How can we see that the victory is final, and the evil is not likely to come back?*
- *Describe the moment (the scene) that demonstrates the change in the protagonist's life after his victory over evil (if shown).*
- *Does this movie show that the hero's ideals are now a reality? If so, how?*

13. Observation: Create the Timeline

- *Create the TIMELINE for the film you have chosen.*

Yes, this is not going to be easy or quick, but this Observation will allow you to see the entire structure of the film. This will help you gain a "professional's point of view.

Would you like to learn how to "see" the structure of successful films? Then do this!

14. Observation: Episode Plan

Create the episode plan for the film you have chosen.

15. Observation: Elements that Advance the Plot

Find the elements that advance the plot in each episode of your episode plan.

16. Observation: List of Episodes

Make a list of all the episodes in the film you have chosen and give them names.

Part 3

1. Observation: Character's Function

Choose three characters from the movie you have just watched.

Describe each of them as follows:

- *What are his intentions?*
- *Does he interfere with the protagonist achieving his goal or does he help him? (Unless this is the protagonist.)*
- *What methods does he use to pursue his intentions?*
- *What is his role in the story?*
- *Why was he introduced into the story?*

_____
_____
_____
_____
_____

2. Observation: Character's Goal

Describe the GOALS of the three characters you have chosen.

3. Observation: Motivation

- *Describe the MOTIVATION of the three characters you have chosen.*
- *Why must each of them perform his function?*
- *WHAt is his reason for that?*
- *Determine whether the motivation of those characters changes as the story unfolds.*

4. Observation: Character's "Heaven"

- *Describe the "HEAVEN" of the characters you have chosen the way you see it.*
- *Answer these questions about each character: What does he dream about? What does he strive for?*

5. Observation: Character's "Hell"

- *Describe the "HELL" of the characters you have chosen the way you see it.*
- *Answer these questions about each character: What is his biggest fear?*
- *What is he trying to avoid at all costs?*
- *What will happen if he doesn't reach his goal or solve the main problem?*

_____
_____
_____
_____
_____
_____
_____
_____
_____
_____
_____

6. Observation: Character's Emotional wound

Describe the emotional wounds of the characters you have chosen.

7. Observation: Internal Conflict

Describe the internal conflicts of the characters you have chosen.

8. Observation: Character's Strengths

- *Describe strong points of the chosen characters.*
- *Determine which of these strong points help each character achieve their goals.*

9. Observation: Character's Weaknesses

- *Describe the weak points of each character you have chosen.*
- *Determine how these weak points impede each character in achieving his goals.*

10. Observation: Character's Characteristics

- *Identify and describe the internal characteristics of each character you have chosen.*
- *Do the internal characteristics influence the story?*
- *Identify and describe the external characteristics of each character.*

11. Observation: External Image

Describe in detail the appearance of the characters you have chosen.

12. Observation: Conflicts

- *Describe the conflicts that involve the characters you have chosen.*
- *Specify the reason for each conflict.*

13. Observation: Character's Personal Growth

- *Determine whether the characters you have chosen experience personal growth. If so, describe it.*
- *Describe the reasons for this personal growth.*

Part 4

1. Observation: The Main Question

Identify and write down the "main question" of the movie.

2. Observation: The Hooks

- *Find and describe the "hooks" in the movie.*
- *Write down the question the viewers are asking themselves as a result of each "hook."*

3. Observation: The Keys

- *Find the "keys" in the movie.*
- *Describe why the protagonist would not be able to move further without at least one of the keys, in other words, why the plot would get stuck in that case.*

4. Observation: Obtaining the Keys

- *Determine which "keys" the protagonist gets easily and which he obtains with great difficulty.*
- *Describe the protagonist's RISK and dangers he had to face in those scenes in which the key was hard to get.*
- *Think of some other ways that would make obtaining the "keys" even more complicated.*

5. Observation: Pressure of Circumstances

Describe how the "increasing pressure of the circumstances" is represented in the movie.

6. Observation: Surprises and Unexpected Twists

Describe the surprises and unexpected twists in the movie.

https://story-flash.com

www.ingramcontent.com/pod-product-compliance
Lightning Source LLC
Chambersburg PA
CBHW071400210526
45465CB00001B/178